HOW TO BE TOTALLY MISERABLE

A Self-Hinder Book

JOHN BYTHEWAY

BOOKCRAFT

SALT LAKE CITY, UTAH

Library of Congress Cataloging-in-Publication Data

Bytheway, John, 1962–
  How to be totally miserable / John Bytheway.
    p.   cm.
  Summary: Presents advice for Mormon teenagers on how to find happiness. Features quotes from various sources, including Mormon teachings.
  ISBN 1-57008-724-5 (hardcover : alk. paper)
  1. Mormon youth—Religious life. 2. Attitude (Psychology)—Religious aspects—Church of Jesus Christ of Latter-day Saints. 3. Mormon youth—Religious life—Humor. 4. Attitude (Psychology—Religious aspects—Church of Jesus Christ of Latter-day Saints—Humor. [1. Attitude (Psychology—Religious aspects—Church of Jesus Christ of Latter-day Saints. 2. Happiness—Religious aspects—Church of Jesus Christ of Latter-day Saints. 3. Conduct of life.] I. Title.
BX8643.Y6. B965 2001
248.8'3—dc21   2001003943

Printed in the United States of America   72876-6866
100 N. Miller Street, Fairfield, PA 17320

10   9   8   7   6   5   4   3

HOW TO BE TOTALLY MISERABLE

Daily, constantly, we choose by our desires, our thoughts, and our actions whether we want to be blessed or cursed, happy or miserable.

—Ezra Taft Benson, *Church News*, April 16, 1988

INTRODUCTION

It has been said that, in this life, suffering is mandatory, but misery is optional.

We all have problems, but we also have a choice. We can choose to be happy, or we can choose to be miserable.

Being miserable requires effort—you must ignore a lot of things you already know are true.

In this little book, you'll learn how to be miserable, and on the way, you'll also learn how not to be. (Miserable, that is . . .)

Real difficulties can be overcome; it is the imaginary ones that are unconquerable.

—Theodore N. Vail, in *The Forbes Book of Business Quotations,* ed. Ted Goodman (Black Dog and Leventhal Publishers, 1997), 205

USE YOUR
IMAGI-NATION TO WORRY

The Imagi-Nation is a little country in your head. When you're young, you go there to play. When you get older, you go there to worry. Worrywarts are mountains on the relief map of the Imagi-Nation. Faith is like Compound W. It is prescription-strength medicine for worrywarts. Joseph Smith taught, "Where doubt and uncertainty are there faith is not, nor can it be. For doubt and faith do not exist in the same person at the same time" (*Lectures on Faith* 6:12). To be miserable, you must visit the Imagi-Nation only to worry. You mustn't go there to plan, dream, ponder, or play. Miserable people go to the Imagi-Nation to act out all the bad things that might happen. No one wants to be around a worrywart, because misery loves company and worrywarts are contagious.

**Tough times never last,
but tough people do!**
—Title of book by Robert Schuller
(Bantam Books, 1983)

BELIEVE THAT THINGS WILL NEVER CHANGE

The sun goes up, and the sun goes down. Seasons come and seasons go. The rain falls in the spring, the summer sun shines, the weather turns cold, clouds gather, and the snow flies. Everything in nature goes through cycles. If you're in the midst of a trial, things will change. If your heart aches, it will heal. Those striving to be miserable must ignore all this. They must believe that things will *never* change, that the sun will *not* come out tomorrow, and that they *don't* deserve a break today. The miserable believe that *nothing ever changes*. (Okay, change the page.)

Everyone can be discontented if he ignores his blessings and looks only at his burdens.

—Thomas S. Monson, *Favorite Quotations from the Collection of Thomas S. Monson* (Deseret Book, 1985), 142

THINK ABOUT YOUR PROBLEMS

In order to be miserable, you're going to have to spend a lot of time thinking about your problems. Sure, there are lots of much more interesting things to think about, like your plans, your goals, your dreams—and when upon life's pillows, you might even count your blessings one by one. But that will only lead to excitement, anticipation, and gratitude. The happiest people think their thoughts according to a plan, and in order to be miserable, you've got to have a plan too—plan to ignore all your wonderful possibilities and ponder only your problems. People eventually become what they think about, so to be miserable, think about your problems until you become one. (Rest assured, however, that someone is going to come along and try to solve you.)

Arise; for this matter belongeth unto thee: . . . be of good courage, and do it.

—Ezra 10:4

DON'T DO ANYTHING

Miserable people wallow. They just sit there. They don't have a "Things to Do" list, they have a "Things to Don't" list. They don't "go and do," they sit and stew. Happy people know that activity and depression are opposites. They're always out doing something. They're making people laugh, and smile, and say "I love that guy." They can't wait to get up in the morning because they have places to go and people to see before they go down at night. In order to be miserable, it's important that you don't have any accomplishments to think about when your head hits the pillow. The motto of the miserable is "Just Don't Do It."

Fear is that little darkroom where negatives are developed.

—Michael Pritchard, in John-Roger and Peter McWilliams, *Do It* (Prelude Press, 1991), 36

WORRY ABOUT THINGS YOU CAN'T CONTROL

There are problems in the Middle East, the killer bees are migrating northward, there's not enough snowpack in the mountains, and the Jazz are out of the playoffs. This is a small list—if you want a bigger one, watch the evening news. Keep a list of all the sad, dismal, sordid, and ugly events so you know exactly how depressed to be. Then you can mope and worry and fret and be glum. If you want to be miserable, worry about things over which you have no control. Happy people do exactly the opposite. They take Joseph Smith's advice (which came from the miserable Liberty Jail): "Therefore, dearly beloved brethren, let us cheerfully do all things that lie in our power; and then may we stand still, with the utmost assurance, to see the salvation of God, and for his arm to be revealed" (D&C 123:17). This approach is the opposite of misery, since it will only lead to Hinckley-esque faith and optimism.

I complained because I had no shoes
until I saw a man who had no feet.

—Sign in a shoe repair shop

COMPLAIN ABOUT YOUR BLESSINGS

Miserable people complain about everything, including their blessings. If their car breaks down, they complain that it isn't new. If their waitress is slow, they complain and withhold a tip. If prophets warn them against dangerous media, they say, "They can't tell me what movies to see." They're like the ancient Israelites who got free food from heaven and said, "What? Manna again?" By contrast, happy people are grateful to have a car, thankful they can afford to eat out at a restaurant (even if service is slow), and prone to sing songs like, "We Thank Thee, O God, for a Prophet." (What good is having a prophet if we don't follow him?) The righteous rejoice while the miserable murmur.

Generally speaking, the most miserable people I know are those who are obsessed with themselves; the happiest people I know are those who lose themselves in the service of others. . . . By and large, I have come to see that if we complain about life, it is because we are thinking only of ourselves.

—Gordon B. Hinckley, *Teachings of Gordon B. Hinckley* (Deseret Book, 1997), 590

THINK ABOUT YOURSELF

Miserable people think about their height, their weight, their hair, their car, their clothes, their nose. They live in a world of their own. They say things like, "but enough about me . . . what do you think about me?" They treat people like things and things like people. They run their own 24-hour self-service station. Happy people know that the key to being happy is making others so. They see every new day as another opportunity to make the world a better place by making a difference to others. Miserable people think of others only when comparing themselves to them. And comparisons make them either vain or bitter (or more miserable).

Your imagination is yours. You can remember the past you choose, rehearse the future you want, and identify with the real and fictional heroes and events of your selection.

—*Do It,* 119

RELIVE YOUR BAD MEMORIES

There you are, faced with a pile of videos labeled "memories," and a mental VCR. What do you play? It depends on whether you're trying to be happy or miserable. If you're trying to be happy, play the ones that give you hope and make you laugh! If you're trying to be miserable, play and replay the tapes of your past mistakes. Relive all the less-than-good times as if they had value. It's a ridiculous strategy, but that's what miserable people do. As with all other video selections, you have a choice. If after repentance the Lord will remember your sins no more (see D&C 58:42), then maybe you don't need to replay them either. Happy people sometimes replay a sad memory, but they have the motto, "be kind, don't rewind." Miserable people watch the tape again and again until they're depressed. They don't realize that their past doesn't define their future.

When people point fingers at someone else, they should remember that three fingers are pointing back at them.

—Old saying

BLAME EVERYONE AND EVERYTHING

Miserable people are medalists at the annual Blame Games. They are world-class winners in whining, bronze medalists in buck-passing, and victors in victimhood. They hurdle their classes and blame their teachers for their grades; they javelin their jobs and blame their genes; they backstroke through their blessings and blame their background; they steeplechase their stewardship and blame the stake. They run an "it's not my fault" marathon, and at the closing ceremony they close their brains. They complain that the world doesn't dedicate itself to making them happy. Their national anthem says, "o'er the land of the free (from responsibility) and the home of the blame."

This one makes a net;
This one stands and wishes.
Would you like to bet
Which one gets the fishes?

—Chinese rhyme, in *Forbes*, 919

There is a God, and he hath created all things, . . . both things to act and things to be acted upon.

—2 Nephi 2:14

DON'T TAKE ANY ACTION

Happy people act. Miserable people are acted upon. Thinking about your problems without doing anything will ensure that you remain miserable and emotionally groggy. People who jog or take a walk around the block know that moving around and getting your blood flowing somehow helps your brain sort out all the stuff that's going on. Sometimes even mowing the lawn is great therapy for getting depression off your turf. Happy people get the sun in their hair and the wind in their face. They listen to the birds and smell the grass, and suddenly things seem a little better. Those who feel miserable inside often stay inside, while those who want to get it out, get out of the house and find something important to do.

It's hard to fight an enemy who has outposts in your head.

—Sally Kempton, in *Do It*, 22

PUT YOURSELF DOWN

Miserable people put themselves down. If you extend a hand to them, they return a backhand. If you pay them a compliment, they give you a refund! They have a "no I'm not" for every "yes you are." It's exhausting to be around them. Every time they put themselves down, you try to lift them up, and the weight becomes too much to bear! Their attitude is not humility, it's humiliating. Happy people know their shortcomings, but they don't sell themselves short. They believe their souls are precious (see Alma 31:35), and when the world weighs them down, they let the Lord lift them up (see Moroni 9:25).

Set . . . goals that you can reach. Set goals that are well balanced—not too many nor too few, and not too high nor too low. Write down your attainable goals and work on them according to their importance. Pray for divine guidance in your goal setting.

—M. Russell Ballard, *Ensign*, May 1987, 14

24

DON'T SET GOALS

If you're trying to be miserable, it's important you don't have any goals. No school goals, personal goals, seminary goals, family goals. With nothing to shoot for, your life is shot. Your only objective each day should be to inhale and exhale for sixteen hours before you go to bed again. Don't read anything informative, don't listen to anything useful, don't do anything productive. If you start achieving goals, you might start to feel a sense of excitement, then you might want to set another goal, and then your miserable mornings are through. To maintain your misery, the idea of crossing off your goals should never cross your mind.

All of us carry excess baggage around from time to time, but the wisest ones among us don't carry it for very long. They get rid of it.

Some of it you have to get rid of without really solving the problem. Some things that ought to be put in order are not put in order because you can't control them.

Often, however, the things we carry are petty, even stupid. If you are still upset after all these years because Aunt Clara didn't come to your wedding reception, why don't you grow up? Forget it.

—Boyd K. Packer, *That All May Be Edified* (Bookcraft, 1982), 68

HOLD ON TO GRUDGES

Okay, everyone out there who needs forgiveness, raise your hands. Hmmm, it appears the voting is unanimous in the affirmative. If you're determined to be miserable, it's important to hold a grudge. Grudges sour your mood and ruin your day. They are part of Satan's plan of misery, because if you don't let go of grudges, you won't be able to hold the rod of iron. The iron rod is the only path that leads to the tree of life "whose fruit is most precious and most desirable above all other fruits" (1 Nephi 15:36). Yes, there are other fruits out there, and the fruit on the thorn bush of grudges is bitter. It's bitter because it prevents you from tasting the greatest fruit of all—the love of God. In other words, no tree-of-life fruit, no eternal life. As someone once said, if we don't forgive, we burn the bridge over which we ourselves must pass!

27

"I can't cheer up—I don't **WANT** to cheer up. It's nicer to be miserable!"

—Anne of Green Gables

It is difficult to make a man miserable while he feels he is worthy of himself and claims kindred to the great God who made him.

—Abraham Lincoln

STAY MISERABLE

Some people are miserable because, well, maybe they enjoy it. Perhaps it's easier to be mad at everyone and everything than to look inside and realize that you don't have to be miserable—or more important, you don't have to *stay* miserable. The fact is, when you get sick and tired of being sick and tired, you'll change. You'll find that it takes work and effort to stay miserable when there's so much to be optimistic about in the world. As Elder M. Russell Ballard once said, "The best thing about living a Christ-centered life, however, is how it makes you feel—inside. It's hard to have a negative attitude about things if and when your life is focused on the Prince of Peace. There will still be problems. Everyone has them. But faith in the Lord Jesus Christ is a power to be reckoned with in the universe and in individual lives" (*Our Search for Happiness* [Deseret Book, 1993], 15).

Who am I to judge another
When I walk imperfectly?

—*Hymns*, no. 220

If we could read the secret history
of our enemies, we should find in each
man's life sorrow and suffering enough
to disarm all hostility.

—Henry Wadsworth Longfellow,
in *Contributor*, July 1882, 312

JUDGE OTHER PEOPLE'S MOTIVES

Miserable people are suspicious. If someone's nice to them, miserable people say, "I wonder why they did that." They look sideways at service and think that angels have an angle. Happy people receive the gift and return gratitude, while the miserable are gracious up front, but wonder what's behind it. Everyone's a suspect, and favors are fishy. They don't realize that the Good Samaritan wasn't performing a service project, he was actually *good!* And he has *good* company today. But, if you'd rather be miserable, then you'll have to go on believing that everyone has an agenda and being a critic of kindness.

I have noticed that folks are just about as happy as they have made up their minds to be.

—Abraham Lincoln

PUT DEADLINES ON YOUR HAPPINESS

Miserable people look for some outside event to make them happy. "As soon as I graduate, I'll be happy." (Then they graduate.) "Well, as soon as I get a job, I'll be happy." (Then they get a job.) "Okay, as soon as I get married, I'll be happy." Miserable people never seem to learn that happiness is a decision, not a destination. It's an attitude, not an event! Nephi was happy while eating raw meat in a desert (see 1 Nephi 17:1–2). If you're determined to be miserable, then think of life as a waiting room, and happiness as your doctor. You know you'll be waiting in there forever, so enjoy the magazines. (And when you finally see the elusive Dr. Happiness, he'll just tell you to schedule another appointment, and *then* you'll be happy.)

Remember that in the end, surely God will be looking only for clean hands, not full ones.

—Jeffrey R. Holland, "Graduation Gifts From the Grave," BYU commencement address, April 26, 1991

A man is rich in proportion to the number of things which he can afford to let alone.

—Henry David Thoreau, in *Do It*, 454

ALWAYS WANT MORE

The miserable think that what they have is never enough. Like the Little Mermaid, who owned no fewer than twenty thingamabobs, they say, "But who cares, no big deal, I want more." (How could you be miserable with twenty thingamabobs and a snarfblat?) The miserable say, "If only I had one of those, I'd be happy." Jesus taught, on the other hand, "Beware of covetousness: for a man's life consisteth not in the abundance of the things which he possesseth" (Luke 12:15). Actually, the more stuff you have, the more stuff you have to worry about. Whatever you obtain, you have to maintain. Clothes attract moths, and cars get rusty, and stuff gets stolen. That's why Jesus said, "Lay up for yourselves treasures in heaven, where neither moth nor rust doth corrupt, and where thieves do not break through nor steal" (3 Nephi 13:20).

I do not know how anybody can feel gloomy for very long who is a member of this Church. Do you feel gloomy? Lift your eyes. Stand on your feet. Say a few words of appreciation and love to the Lord. Be positive.

—Gordon B. Hinckley, *Teachings*, 412–13

BE A BREATH OF STALE AIR

Some people are fun to be around. When they enter the room, they're like the proverbial "breath of fresh air." The miserable, on the other hand, can find a way to be the slug of the party. They seem to delight in "throwing a wrench in the works," "putting a damper on things," and even interrupting the Sunday School teacher to be the "devil's advocate." (Be serious, who would ever want to be known as the devil's advocate?) No activity is fun enough, no dance has the right music, and no lesson is sufficiently entertaining. You wish they'd just keep their mouths closed, because all that comes out is stale air (and they're out of Tic Tacs).

Man's mind, once stretched by a new idea, never regains its original dimensions.

—Oliver Wendell Holmes

DON'T LEARN ANYTHING NEW

Happy people love to learn. Miserable people think learning is just too much work. Happy people love getting up in the morning and knowing that, in the day ahead, they will learn many new things they didn't know when they got up. Happy people are interested, inquisitive, and inspiring. They're also intelligent, because when you ask a lot of questions, you're bound to learn something. Miserable people would rather lounge than learn. They use their drive time to tune in to trash, while the happy turn their cars into classrooms. The miserable read only what they have to for the test, and they'd rather take naps than take notes.

If prayer is only a spasmodic cry at the time of crisis, then it is utterly selfish, and we come to think of God as a repairman or a service agency to help us only in our emergencies.

—Howard W. Hunter, *Ensign,* November 1977, 52

Pray always, and I will pour out my Spirit upon you, and great shall be your blessing—yea, even more than if you should obtain treasures of earth and corruptibleness to the extent thereof.

—D&C 19:38

POSTPONE PRAYER

The happiest people pray early and often, while the miserable often postpone prayer to be used as a last resort. Happy people keep in touch; miserable people keep their distance. A teenage girl in a testimony meeting once said, "Prayer is so easy to stop and so hard to start again—but operators are standing by." In prayer we are never alone, because God plus one other person is a majority, and "if God be for us, who can prevail against us?" (JST, Romans 8:31). Sometimes just knowing the Lord is there and watching over us is a great remedy for misery. President Wilford Woodruff said, "We should call upon the Lord in mighty prayer, and make all our wants known unto him. For if he does not protect and deliver us and save us, no other power will" (*Millennial Star,* 48:806). Happy people stand tallest when they're on their knees, but the miserable haven't got a prayer.

[The Devil] seeketh that all men might be miserable like unto himself.

—2 Nephi 2:27

AVOID GOOD COMPANY

Elder Robert D. Hales once said that a friend is someone who makes it easier to live the gospel (see *Ensign,* May 1990, 40). Happy people build, lift, encourage, and motivate, and being in their company always makes you want to be better too. Since the gospel is the ultimate guide to peace and joy, people who are trying to be miserable would try to find friends who would weigh them down with gloom and doubt and sin. Misery loves this kind of company. Bad company resides in the great and spacious building. They tell you there's something wrong with being good, so they go to the windows and point (see 1 Nephi 8:33). They take you to places you shouldn't be and tempt you to do things you shouldn't do. Then, after you've followed their plan of misery, you feel empty inside, and you wonder why you're miserable! Well, perhaps bad feelings accompany bad company.

I know only two tunes: One of them is "Yankee Doodle" and the other isn't.

—Ulysses S. Grant, in *Forbes*, 601

There is no music in hell, for all good music belongs to heaven.

—Brigham Young, *Journal of Discourses*, 9:244

Sing, O heavens; and be joyful, O earth; and break forth into singing, O mountains: for the Lord hath comforted his people, and will have mercy upon his afflicted.

—Isaiah 49:13

DON'T SING

Aria hungry? Let's eat overture place. Sonata bad idea. There's something about singing a song that makes you happy. If happy people have sunshine in their souls, then miserable people must have a black hole in theirs (people who read a lot of books have chicken soup in their souls). Have you ever seen a depressed person sing? Miserable people sing the blues, while happy people sing "Blue Skies Shinin' on Me." Happy people sing in the shower, sing in the car, even whistle while they work. The Lord said, "The song of the righteous is a prayer unto me" (D&C 25:12). Happy people sing "Zippadee doo dah" while the miserable zippadee up their mouths.

It takes sixty-four muscles of the face to make a frown, and only thirteen to make a smile. Why work overtime?

—"Gems of Thought," *Improvement Era*, June 1923

And it came to pass that Jesus blessed them as they did pray unto him; and his countenance did smile upon them.

—3 Nephi 19:25

DON'T SMILE

If you're trying to be miserable, don't smile. Someone once joked that longtime BYU football coach LaVell Edwards is always smiling inside, he just forgot to tell his face. A clever bumper sticker says, "Put a smile on your kisser, and someone may put a kiss on your smiler." (I think I'll put that on the bathroom mirror and see if my wife gets the hint.) I always thought it would be fun to have a daughter named "Hope" so I could come home and say, "There is Hope smiling brightly before us." I also read in the paper that it's a psychological fact that smiling on the outside makes you feel better on the inside (if it's in the paper, it must be true). Just remember, "to be carnally-minded is death, and to be **Spiritually Minded Is Life Eternal**" ☺ (2 Nephi 9:39).

I am perfectly satisfied that my Father and my God is a cheerful, pleasant, lively, good-natured Being. Why? Because I am cheerful, pleasant, lively, and good-natured when I have His Spirit.

—*Journal of Discourses*, 4:222

When I was attending college, I enrolled in a physiology class. One day during a lecture the professor asked me to sit up on the high table at the front of the room so he could demonstrate the principle of reflexes. He took a little mallet, similar to the one a medical doctor would use, and proceeded to tap me on the knee, expecting my leg to jerk noticeably in typical reflex action. However, I held my leg very rigid and flipped my arm in the air when he tapped my knee. The class roared with delight. The professor was not amused.

—Boyd K. Packer, *Teach Ye Diligently* (Deseret Book, 1975), 251

DON'T LAUGH

Miserable people don't laugh. It might break their concentration! They have important world issues to worry about. Happy people giggle, guffaw, chortle, snicker, and even snort. (Following a snort, they cover their mouths in surprise and embarrassment; then they laugh even harder.) If laughter is the best medicine, these people have free refills at the funny pharmacy. Have you ever laughed so hard that your stomach was sore the next day? There's a great idea for a new exercise video in there somewhere: "Laugh Your Way to Washboard Abs" or something. Now, that's my kind of spa. Comedians could line up at Gold's Gym and tell jokes. In the other places, people just lift weights and grunt and perspire in fashionable Spandex.

The primary reason we are commanded to avoid criticism is to preserve our own spiritual well-being, not to protect the person whom we would criticize.

—Dallin H. Oaks, *Ensign,* February 1987, 68.

Your criticism may be worse than the conduct you are trying to correct.

—James E. Faust, *Ensign,* November 1987, 35.

BACKBITE

Miserable people backbite. They haven't learned that if you want to be big, you shouldn't belittle. Happy people have learned that there is no nobility in confessing the faults of other people behind their backs. Besides, backbiting leaves a bad taste in your mouth. Happy people know that with the same judgment they judge, they will also be judged (see Matthew 7:2). They speak of what's right with others instead of what's wrong. They'd rather lighten the load on the backs of others than bite them. Joseph Smith taught, "The nearer we get to our heavenly Father, the more we are disposed to look with compassion on perishing souls; we feel that we want to take them upon our shoulders, and cast their sins behind our backs" (*Teachings of the Prophet Joseph Smith,* 240–41). Happy people keep their teeth to themselves.

Love not sleep,
lest thou come to poverty.

—Proverbs 20:13

Some dream of big things,
others wake up and do them.

—Old saying

SLEEP LONGER
THAN IS NEEDFUL

Miserable people think they can escape their problems by sleeping. They think the perfect world is only found on their Perfect Sleeper (that's a mattress brand). Happy people know that one of the purposes of life is to matter—and you can't matter much when you're merged with your mattress. Miserable people repeatedly hit the snooze button to avoid living each day to the fullest. When life's alarm clock goes off and says, "Get up and do something," they smack the snooze button and say, "Yeah, sometime I will." At the judgment day, when the Lord asks them, "What did you do with your life?" they'll say, "Well, um, I was kinda tired."

The world turns aside to let any man pass who knows whither he is going.

—David Starr Jordan, in "Notes," *Improvement Era,* August 1901

DON'T HAVE A PURPOSE

Happy people don't get down, because they have a reason to get up. They know why they're here and what they're supposed to do. Since they have a purpose, they live their life *on purpose*. They study their scriptures, memorize their patriarchal blessings, and always seem to be going someplace. Having a purpose is like a rudder that steers you through life's bad weather. Joseph Smith said, "You know, brethren, that a very large ship is benefited very much by a very small helm in the time of a storm, by being kept workways with the wind and the waves" (D&C 123:16). Without a godly purpose, one could be "led about by Satan, even as . . . a vessel is tossed about upon the waves, without sail or anchor, or without anything wherewith to steer her" (Mormon 5:18). Miserable people have no plans, no goals, no dreams, no purpose. No wonder they're miserable!

The past is behind; learn from it.
The future is ahead; prepare for it.
The present is here; live in it!

—Thomas S. Monson, *Favorite Quotations*, 140

Regret is an appalling waste of energy;
you can't build on it; it's only good for
wallowing in.

—Katherine Mansfield, *Forbes*, 778

RECYCLE REGRETS

Miserable people have a recycle bin full of past mistakes. Every day they rethink their regrets and recycle their remorse. Their language is full of phrases like, "I should've," "I would've," "Why didn't I," and "If only." They never look where they're going because they can't take their eyes off where they've been. Happy people know that you can either learn from the past or live in it. (The past is a nice place to visit, but you wouldn't want to live there.) Happy people would rather move on than move in. They turn every regret into a resolve. Rather than saying, "I can't believe I did that," they repent, refocus, and say, "Whew. I'll never do that again!"

Therefore, fear not, little flock; do good; let earth and hell combine against you, for if ye are built upon my rock, they cannot prevail. . . . Look unto me in every thought; doubt not, fear not.

—D&C 6: 34, 36

For God hath not given us the spirit of fear; but of power, and of love, and of a sound mind.

—2 Timothy 1:7

Our doubts are traitors, and make us lose the good we oft might win by fearing to attempt.

—William Shakespeare, *Measure for Measure*, act 1, scene 4, lines 77–79

TAKE COUNSEL
FROM YOUR FEARS

Miserable people always think about what might go wrong. They plan their actions based on their fears. The best they can do is imagine all the worst-case scenarios of what might happen. This is a recipe for misery. Someone once said that FEAR means *False Expectations Appearing Real*. Very often, the things we fear might happen, never do. Throughout the scriptures, when angels come to earth, they almost always begin their message by saying, "Fear not." I guess it would be pretty frightening to see an angel, but maybe there's something more. Perhaps there's a message about faith in there. Think about it. Angels come from this celestial, heavenly place, and the first thing out of their mouth is, "Fear not," as if to say, "You people down on earth are always afraid."

Blessed is he or she who avoids being offended.

—Marvin J. Ashton, *Ensign*, May 1988, 62

Has somebody offended you in the Church? You may hold resentment if you wish, say nothing to him, and let resentment canker your soul. If you do, you will be the one who will be injured, not the one who you think has injured you. You will feel better and be far happier to follow the divine injunction: If you have aught against your brother, go to him. (See Matt. 5:23–24.)

—David O. McKay, *Gospel Ideals*
(Improvement Era, 1953), 258

BE EASILY OFFENDED

Miserable people take offense. If you say something, it offends them. If you don't say something, it offends them. They're mad when someone tries to help, and they're mad when someone doesn't. They're even offended when someone is trying to make amends! They're offended if someone apologizes too late, too quickly, or not enough. (They might even be offended if someone writes a book about being miserable. Uh-oh.) The happiest people in the world forgive quickly because they know they will also need forgiveness. Elder Dallin H. Oaks said, "One of the most Godlike expressions of the human soul is the act of forgiveness. . . . Forgiveness is mortality's mirror image of the mercy of God" (*Ensign,* November 1989, 66). We all need mercy, and being offended isn't the way to get it. Jesus said, "Blessed are the merciful: for they shall obtain mercy" (Matthew 5:7).

I couldn't wait for success, so I went
ahead without it.

—Jonathan Winters, *Bits & Pieces*, May 22, 1997, 3

WAIT FOR LIFE TO HAPPEN

Miserable people are waiting for the world to make them happy. They think there's something wrong if people and things and circumstances aren't going to great lengths to ensure their happiness. Miserable teenagers sit in the foyer during church and expect the ward to entertain them. But happy people know that the responsibility for being happy is on their own shoulders. They understand the old Chinese proverb, "He who waits for roast duck to fly into mouth must wait a very long time." If you want life to give you a roast duck, or even a small order of fries, you've got to go out and get it. Happiness doesn't deliver. You have to get off the couch and go after it!

Life is either a daring adventure, or nothing.

—Helen Keller, in *Forbes*, 523

AVOID ADVENTURE

When you ask miserable people, "What's new?" they say, "Nothing." Miserable people haven't done anything new in years. Happy people love to try new things. And when they encounter a problem, they think of it as just another adventure. If they get lost on their way somewhere, they say, "All right, an adventure!" When the power goes out, they gather the flashlights and tell stories on the couch. If they get caught in a cloudburst, they jump in puddles and sing in the rain! Miserable people, on the other hand, don't see an opportunity for adventure, they just think they're being oppressed. They ask, "What did I do to deserve this?" or "Why does this always happen to me?" (Oh be serious, does this *always* happen to you?) Happy people turn little adversities into big adventures.

At the moment of depression, if you will follow a simple program, you will get out of it. Get on your knees and get the help of God, then get up and go find somebody who needs something that you can help them with. Then it will be a good day.

—Marion D. Hanks, *BYU Speeches of the Year,*
1966, 6–7

No one is useless in this world who lightens the burdens of it for another.

—Charles Dickens, in *Forbes,* 203

ASSUME THAT MOPING WILL SOLVE THE PROBLEM

Miserable people figure that if they lie around, and stew, and think, and nap, and remove themselves from the world, eventually their doing nothing will solve the problem. Happy people know that misery exits when you enter the life of someone else and make a difference. Ironically, one of the best ways to lift your spirits is forget yourself and lift someone else's. And, if you'd like a double dose of depression-destroying activity, do something for someone else *anonymously.* There's a certain giggly giddiness that comes your way when you commit random acts of kindness and nobody knows who did it. It's hard to keep frowning when you know someone else is smiling because of you.

The heaviest load we feel is often from the weight of our unkept promises and our unresolved sins, which press down relentlessly upon us.

—Neal A. Maxwell, *Ensign*, November 1989, 85

I readily confess that I would find no peace, neither happiness nor safety, in a world without repentance. I do not know what I should do if there were no way for me to erase my mistakes. The agony would be more than I could bear.

—Boyd K. Packer, *Ensign*, May 1988, 71

I have never seen happier people than those who have repented.

—Stephen L Richards, in Conference Report, October 1940, 35

PROCRASTINATE REPENTANCE

Miserable people procrastinate repentance. They'd rather put off confession than put off the natural man. Happy people are eager to repent. They can't wait to get rid of the weight.

Perhaps miserable people have the mistaken idea that the choice is between repenting and not repenting. It isn't. The choice is to either repent or suffer (see D&C 19:17). Besides, delaying repentance brings its own kind of suffering. Some people carry burdens for years that could have been lightened by repentance. Boyd K. Packer said, "Often, very often, we are punished as much by our sins as we are for them" (*Teach Ye Diligently*, 310). Miserable people think there's no hurry, while the happiest people hurry up and lighten up.

He who reads it [the scriptures] oftenest will like it best.

—Joseph Smith, *Teachings,* 56

The iron rod does not go through the lobby of the great and spacious building.

—W. Jeffrey Marsh

And I said unto them that it was the word of God; and whoso would hearken unto the word of God, and would hold fast unto it, they would never perish; neither could the temptations and the fiery darts of the adversary overpower them unto blindness, to lead them away to destruction.

—I Nephi 15:24

AVOID SCRIPTURE STUDY

Would you like to know how to act in this drama called life? Well, study the script! But beware, there are false scripts and true scripts. If you want to be miserable, audition for a worldly play with a false script. The world's scripts promote materialism, fame, and popularity. False scripts lead you inside a great and spacious building, leaving you with a great and spacious emptiness inside. True scripts lead to joy. We call them *sure* scripts, or scriptures. There are millions of false scripts out there, but there is only one sure script—the iron rod. There is no substitute iron rod. Those who hearken and hold fast to the iron rod will *never* perish (1 Nephi 15:24), and eventually, they will meet the Author of the sure scripts. C. S. Lewis spoke of the Second Coming when he said, "When the Author of the play comes on stage, the play is over!" (as quoted by Neal A. Maxwell, *New Era,* January 1971, 9).